Good Food
+ Good Friends
—————————————
A Good Life
Happy Cooking!
S.C. Hatch

A Cookbook with Options

3 Methods of Cooking Each Recipe
Stove/Oven, Slow Cooker or Instant Pot

S.C. Hatch

LifeRich Publishing is a registered trademark of The Reader's Digest Association, Inc.

LifeRich Publishing books may be ordered through booksellers or by contacting:

LifeRich Publishing
1663 Liberty Drive
Bloomington, IN 47403
www.liferichpublishing.com
1 (888) 238-8637

ISBN: 978-1-4897-1726-9 (sc)
ISBN: 978-1-4897-1727-6 (hc)
ISBN: 978-1-4897-1725-2 (e)

Library of Congress Control Number: 2018945134

Print information available on the last page.

LifeRich Publishing rev. date: 6/19/2018

Dedication

This cookbook is dedicated to my grandma, Esther Radabah. She gave me a love for good food, good friends, and family; and showed me how those ingredients make a great life

Foreword

I grew up in Montana, where country is a way of life, which begins in the kitchen. My fondest memories are the moments I spent in my grandma's kitchen. It was always the place to be. Laughter and people telling stories was such a draw, along with the smell of great food.

My grandma taught me to bake and gave me a love for homemade cookies. I am happiest when I am making homemade cookies and thinking about those wonderful childhood memories.

When I got married, I was a bit surprised to learn that I would be cooking every day. I was a little intimidated, having watched my Mom make meals, without a recipe, knowing I couldn't possibly do it that way. Luckily, someone gave me a 6-ingredient or less cookbook as a wedding present. I soon learned that I could follow a recipe well, and thought there was hope of surviving the task. Well, that was nearly 30 years ago now. I love how good meals bring joy to my family, and friends, and how those moments around good food are where memories are made.

I am always looking for ways to make the daily cooking routine easier, without compromising on taste. Recently, I started noticing that I was making the same meal in different ways, depending on the schedule, and the time I had to put towards cooking. Sometimes, I wanted to put the meal in the slow cooker, work all day, and come home to dinner. Other times I needed a meal quick, and would use the *Instant Pot*. Then there would be times where I had the time and energy to make the meal traditionally on the stove or in the oven. As I was collecting recipes, cooked different ways, the idea for this cookbook was born.

I hope you like the recipes, and use the options provided. Most of all, I hope you are filled with joy, and sit with your family, as you enjoy your meals together.

Happy cooking!
Shawntel Hatch

Introduction

In general, I have found that meals prepared with the traditional method seem the freshest. Meals prepared in the slow cooker generally have the best flavor. Meals prepared in the *Instant Pot* are cooked to perfection, but getting the right amount of flavor is a challenge because of how quickly the food cooks, which is why sautéing the flavors first becomes an important step. All the recipes are tested on a 6-quart *Instant Pot*. I like having options for the same recipe so I can use whatever methods work for my schedule. The photos of the food are meant to give you an idea of what your dish might look like. I purposely did not take high quality photos because I wanted this cookbook to feel like anyone with any skill level in the kitchen can be successful using these recipes. I hope this cookbook makes it easier for you to cook at home.

Breakfast

In this section, I would like to share some recipe options for the morning meal. I like to do simple homemade breakfast options during the week. Egg muffins, or hard-boiled eggs and bacon are our favorite "go to" recipes. French toast, steel cut oats, or Hawaiian breakfast rice can be made on the weekend and warmed up during the week. I also use leftover red potatoes and warm them up for breakfast with a scrambled egg or two on top.

- Egg muffins
- French toast
- Hawaiian breakfast rice
- Hard boiled eggs
- Steel cut oats
- Biscuits and gravy

Egg Muffins in the Oven

Why drive through Starbucks when you can make egg muffins yourself? These are fast, easy, and delicious; high in protein and so versatile.

Prep time is 10-20 minutes, cook time is 17 minutes. 4 servings.

Basic Ingredients

- 6 eggs
- ½ c half-n-half or milk
- ¼ tsp pepper
- 1/8 tsp red pepper (optional) Red pepper gives the eggs additional flavor so they aren't so bland.

Versatile Ingredients

- ½ c fruit or cooked vegetable
- ½ c cheese
- ½ c cooked meat

My favorite combination is sautéed yellow onion, bacon bits, and Gruyere cheese. You could easily do Swiss cheese instead of Gruyere cheese. Second runner up is pineapple, diced ham, and Cheddar cheese. I also like to line the muffin cups with crushed nacho *Doritos* and make them with tomatoes, Pepper Jack cheese, and sausage. You may top them with salsa and sour cream.

Instructions:

Preheat oven to 400 degrees. Spray a 12-cup muffin pan with cooking spray. Mix ingredients in a bowl. I find that a large cookie scoop works the best for filling the muffin cups with the mixture. Cook for 17 minutes. Cool for at least 5 minutes and enjoy. Egg muffins can be refrigerated and warmed up. Serve with homemade English muffin bread, jam, and fresh squeezed orange juice for a real treat.

Egg Muffins in the Slow Cooker

You can make these in the slow cooker too.
Prep time is still 10-20 minutes; 1 – 1 ½ hours cook time.
1-2 servings.

Basic Ingredients

- 4 eggs
- 5 T and 1 tsp half-n-half or milk
- 1/8 tsp black pepper
- Smidge of red pepper (optional) for flavoring

Versatile Ingredients

- 5 T and 1 tsp fruit or cooked vegetable
- 5 T and 1 tsp cheese
- 5 T and 1 tsp cooked meat

My favorite combination is sautéed yellow onion, bacon bits, and Gruyere cheese. You could easily do Swiss cheese instead of Gruyere cheese. Second runner up is pineapple, diced ham, and Cheddar cheese. I also like to line the muffin cups with crushed nacho *Doritos* and make them with tomatoes, Pepper Jack cheese, and sausage. You can top them with salsa and sour cream.

Instructions:

Preheat slow cooker on high (can take up to an hour). Spray a 4-cup silicon muffin pan with cooking spray. Mix ingredients in a bowl, and then use a large cookie scoop to scoop the mixture into the muffin tins. Set muffin pan in slow cooker insert and prop lid open for the steam to escape. Cook on high for 1 – 1 ½ hours. It is important to turn the muffin pan halfway through the baking time because one side of the slow cooker is hotter than the other side. Cool for at least 5 minutes and enjoy. Egg muffins can be refrigerated and warmed up. Serve with homemade English muffin bread, jam, and fresh squeezed orange juice for a real treat.

Egg Muffins in the Instant Pot

These are fast and easily done in the *Instant Pot*. 10-20 minutes prep time; 8 minutes of cook time. 1-2 servings.

Basic Ingredients

- 4 eggs
- 5 T and 1 tsp half-n-half or milk
- 1/8 tsp black pepper
- Smidge of red pepper (optional) for flavoring

Versatile Ingredients

- 5 T and 1 tsp fruit or cooked vegetable
- 5 T and 1 tsp cheese
- 5 T and 1 tsp cooked meat

My favorite combination is sautéed yellow onion, bacon bits, and Gruyere cheese. You could easily do Swiss cheese instead of Gruyere cheese. Second runner up is pineapple, diced ham, and Cheddar cheese. I also like to line the muffin cups with crushed nacho *Doritos* and make them with tomatoes, Pepper Jack cheese, and sausage. You may also top them with salsa and sour cream.

Instructions:

Put a trivet in the *Instant Pot* with 1 ½ cups of water. Spray a 4-cup muffin pan with cooking spray. Mix ingredients in a bowl, and then use a large cookie scoop to scoop the batter into the muffin tin. Cook for 8 minutes on manual. Wait 2 minutes and do a quick release. Open the lid, remove the muffin cups. Cool for at least 5 minutes and enjoy. Egg muffins can be refrigerated and warmed up. Serve with homemade English muffin bread, jam, and fresh squeezed orange juice for a real treat.

French Toast on the Stove

French Toast is a classic breakfast dish. You can freeze leftovers with wax paper between the bread pieces and warm up during the week. I like to make my French toast with homemade cinnamon swirl bread. I also really love the tropical version for something unique.
30 minutes prep time and 10-15 minutes of cook time. Serves 4.

Ingredients

- 8 slices thick sandwich bread (You can also use cinnamon swirl bread)
- 6 eggs
- 1 c heavy cream, half-n-half or milk
- 1 T vanilla
- 1 T maple syrup
- 1 T coconut rum (optional)
- 1 tsp cinnamon
- 1/8 tsp nutmeg
- ¼ tsp salt
- butter
- ½ c chopped macadamia nuts (optional)
- ¼ c coconut (optional)

Instructions:

Mix eggs, cream, vanilla, cinnamon, nutmeg, salt, sugar, maple syrup, and coconut rum, if using. Place bread in shallow baking dish in single layer and pour egg mixture over the bread. Let sit for 10 minutes. Turn bread over and let sit for 10 more minutes. Put a baking pan with a wire rack in the oven on 200 degrees. Add 1 T butter to a frying pan on medium heat. Fry French toast 2-3 minutes on each side. Transfer to warm oven. Serve. You can top with macadamia nuts, coconut, caramel syrup, or maple syrup, powdered sugar, and fruit.

French Toast in the Slow Cooker

My family thinks this dish tastes exceptional cooked in the slow cooker with homemade cinnamon swirl bread.

Prep time 30 minutes and cook time 2-4 hours. Serves 4.

Ingredients

- 8 slices thick sandwich bread (You can also use cinnamon swirl bread)
- 6 eggs
- 2 c heavy cream, half-n-half or milk
- 1 T vanilla
- 1 T maple syrup
- 1 T coconut rum (optional)
- 1 tsp cinnamon
- 1/8 tsp nutmeg
- ¼ tsp salt
- ½ c dark brown sugar
- ¼ c butter softened
- ½ c chopped macadamia nuts (optional)
- ¼ c coconut (optional)

Instructions:

Cube bread and place on baking sheet. Bake at 300 degrees for 8-10 minutes to dry out. Mix eggs, cream, vanilla, cinnamon, nutmeg, salt, maple syrup and coconut rum, if using. Place cooled bread crumbs in a bowl and toss with egg mixture. Coat a slow cooker insert with cooking spray, or line with a slow cooker liner. Add bread cubes to slow cooker. Cover and place in fridge for 4 hours. Cream brown sugar and butter together and add to the top of the bread cubes. Sprinkle with macadamia nuts and coconut, if using. Cook on high for 2 hours, or low for 4 hours. You may serve with maple syrup or caramel syrup.

French Toast in the Instant Pot

You can use the *Instant Pot* in slow cooker mode to make these. Prep time 20 minutes. Cook time 1 ½ hours. Serves 4.

Ingredients

- 8 slices thick sandwich bread (You can also use cinnamon swirl bread)
- 6 eggs
- 2 c heavy cream, half-n-half or milk
- 1 T vanilla
- 1 T maple syrup
- 1 T coconut rum (optional)

- 1 tsp cinnamon
- 1/8 tsp nutmeg
- ¼ tsp salt
- ½ c dark brown sugar
- ¼ c butter softened
- ½ c chopped macadamia nuts (optional)
- ¼ c coconut (optional)

Instructions:

Coat inner pot with cooking spray. Mix eggs, cream, vanilla, cinnamon, nutmeg, salt, maple syrup, and coconut rum, if using. Cut bread into 1-inch cubes and bake in 300-degree oven for 8-10 minutes. Place cooled bread crumbs in a bowl and toss with egg mixture. Add bread to the pot. Cream butter and sugar together and add to the bread crumbs. Sprinkle with macadamia nuts and coconut, if using. Place a 10 ½ inch piece of aluminum foil on top of inner pot. Tuck under pot. Cut 1-inch slits in foil at 12, 3, 6, and 9 o'clock 1 inch from edge. Cut a second slit 1-inch to the inside of the first slit 1 ¼ inch long. Close and lock the lid. Turn the steam release handle to venting. Press slow cook and choose 1 hour 30 minutes cook time. You may serve warm with maple syrup or caramel syrup, or powdered sugar and fruit.

Hawaiian Breakfast Rice on the Stove

I first had this dish at a local café on Maui, Hawaii, with Spam. I prefer to make it with bacon. Look for fresh pineapple from Hawaii or the tropics for better flavor. Prep time 10-15 minutes. Cook time 15-20 minutes. Serves 4.

Ingredients

- 4 tsp olive oil
- ½ c chopped red onion
- 1 bunch green onion chopped separate the white parts and the green parts
- ½ c chopped macadamia nuts (optional)
- 1 tsp minced garlic
- 4 c cooked rice

- 1 c chopped fresh Hawaiian Pineapple or 1 c drained pineapple tidbits in a pinch
- 1 c bacon bits
- 3 T tamari sauce
- 1 tsp toasted sesame oil
- 2 tsp dark brown sugar
- ½ tsp ground ginger
- 4 eggs

Instructions:

Mix the tamari sauce, sesame oil, brown sugar, and ground ginger. Heat frying pan on medium heat. Add the olive oil. Sauté the macadamia nuts for a minute, if using, and remove nuts to a paper towel lined plate. Sauté the red onion, and white parts of the green onions, until tender. Add the garlic and cook for 30 seconds. Add the rice and bacon and cook until heated through. Add the liquid, green onions, and pineapple. Stir until combined. Add macadamia nuts back in, if using. Cover and reduce to very low heat to keep warm. In a separate pan, cook eggs as you like - scrambled or fried. I like to put the rice mixture in a bowl, and then put it on the plate in a mound, and then top with eggs.

Hawaiian Breakfast Rice in the Slow Cooker

If you have the time, this dish is easiest in the Slow Cooker and tastes great.

Prep time 10-15 minutes. Cook time 2-4 hours. Serves 4.

Ingredients

- ½ c chopped red onion
- 1 bunch green onion chopped separate the white parts and the green parts
- 1 tsp minced garlic
- 4 c cooked jasmine rice
- 1 c chopped fresh Hawaiian Pineapple or 1 c drained pineapple tidbits in a pinch
- 1 c bacon bits

- ¼ c water
- 3 T tamari sauce
- 1 tsp toasted sesame oil
- 2 tsp dark brown sugar
- ½ tsp ground ginger
- ½ c chopped macadamia nuts (optional)
- 4 eggs

Instructions:

Line a 6-qt slow cooker with a slow cooker liner, or coat the slow cooker with cooking spray. Put the rice, red onions, white part of the green onions, and bacon bits in the slow cooker. Mix together the water, tamari sauce, sesame oil, brown sugar, ginger, and garlic. Pour over the rice mixture and cook on high 2-3 hours, or low for 3-4 hours. Add the green part of the green onions, pineapple and macadamia nuts, if using. Cook eggs, fried or scrambled, and serve on top the rice.

Hawaiian Breakfast Rice in the Instant Pot

This dish is surprisingly easy to do in the *Instant Pot*.
Prep time 10-15 minutes. Cook time 10 minutes. Serves 4.

Ingredients

- 4 tsp olive oil
- ½ c chopped red onion
- 1 bunch green onion chopped separate the white parts and the green parts
- ½ c chopped macadamia nuts (optional)
- 1 tsp minced garlic
- 2 c jasmine rice
- 2 c water
- 1 c chopped fresh Hawaiian Pineapple or 1 c drained pineapple tidbits in a pinch
- 1 c bacon bits
- 3 T tamari sauce
- 1 tsp toasted sesame oil
- 2 tsp dark brown sugar
- ½ tsp ground ginger
- 4 eggs

Instructions:

Mix the tamari sauce, sesame oil, brown sugar, and ground ginger together. Press sauté mode on the *Instant Pot*. When hot, add the olive oil and macadamia nuts, if using. Cook for 1 minute. Remove nuts to a paper towel lined plate. Add the red onion and white onion parts to the *Instant Pot* and cook until tender. Add the garlic and cook for 10 seconds. Add the rice and cook for 1 minute. Turn off. Add the water and the liquid mixture. Put the lid on and set on manual for 10 minutes. When the Instant Pot dings, let sit on warm for 5 minutes. Cook the eggs the way you like them, fried or scrambled, on the stove while the rice is cooking in the *Instant Pot*. Turn *Instant Pot* off. Quick release. Add the bacon, macadamia nuts, if using, and pineapple, stir and serve with the eggs.

Hard Boiled Eggs on the Stove

One of our favorite weekday breakfast meals is bacon, and hard-boiled eggs. Bacon is super easy to cook in the oven. For thick sliced bacon, line baking sheet with foil and insert wire rack. Lay bacon on wire rack and broil for 3 minutes. Turn bacon over and broil for 2-3 more minutes. Hard boiled eggs can be rough to get just right. This is the only stove top method that has worked for me.

Prep time 5 minutes. Cook time 15 minutes.

Ingredients

- Eggs
- Water

Instructions:

Place eggs in pan and cover with cold water. Choose a cooking pan that will hold the amount of eggs you are cooking, with the least amount of extra space, for the eggs to click together. You don't want your eggs cracking while they are boiling. Heat on medium-high heat until the water boils. Continue to boil for 15 minutes, adjusting the heat so the eggs don't click together and crack. After the eggs have been simmering in a slow boil for 15 minutes, transfer pan to sink and fill pan with ice and cold water so the eggs stop cooking. Allow to sit in the ice water for at least 5 minutes. Peel and enjoy.

Hard Boiled Eggs in the Slow Cooker

The slow cooker is a great way to cook a lot of eggs at one time.
Prep time 5 minutes. Cook time 3 ½ hours.

Ingredients

*   Eggs
*   Water

Instructions:

Place eggs in slow cooker and cover with water. Cook on low for 3 ½ hours. Transfer eggs to bowl filled with ice and water. Allow to sit in the ice water for 5 minutes. Peel and enjoy.

Hard Boiled Eggs in the Instant Pot

This is my favorite way of cooking hard boiled eggs. They cook perfectly and are easy to peel. Prep time 5 minutes. Cook time 6 minutes.

Ingredients
- Eggs
- Water

Instructions:

Pour 1 cup of water in bottom of *Instant Pot*. Insert whatever device you are using to hold the eggs. The device I used in the picture is an egg stand for the *Instant Pot*. Instead of the egg stand, you can use your trivet and some heat proof cups, to hold the eggs apart from each other, so they don't crack. Place whatever amount of eggs you want to cook in the *Instant Pot*. Secure the lid and close the steam valve. Press steam setting and adjust the time to 6 minutes unless you want to have runny yolks, then press 4 minutes. When the *Instant Pot,* dings, let the eggs natural release for 6 minutes. Quick release whatever steam is left. Transfer eggs to a bowl that has ice and water in it. Let sit in ice bath for 6 minutes. Peel and enjoy.

Steel Cut Oats on the Stove

To me, oatmeal done with steel cut oats tastes better than oatmeal flakes.

Prep time 5 minutes. Cook time 30 minutes. Serves 4.

Ingredients

- 1 c steel cut oats
- 3 c water
- 1 c milk
- ¼ tsp salt

Instructions:

Bring water and milk to a boil over medium heat. Add oats and salt and simmer on low for 30 minutes. Take pan off heat and let sit for 5 minutes. Serve with your favorite toppings. Our favorites are pumpkin puree, pecans, and pumpkin pie seasoning; or dried pineapple, macadamia nuts and coconut.

Steel Cut Oats in the Slow Cooker

If you have the time, cooking oatmeal in the slow cooker tastes the best to my family.

Prep time 5 minutes. Cook time 4-6 hours. Serves 4.

Ingredients

- 1 c steel cut oats
- 3 c water
- 1 c milk
- 1/2 tsp salt

Instructions:

Combine ingredients in slow cooker. Cook on low 4-6 hours. Let cool 10 minutes. Fluff and serve with your favorite toppings. Our favorite toppings are pumpkin puree, pecans, and pumpkin pie seasoning; or dried pineapple, macadamia nuts and coconut.

Steel Cut Oats in the Instant Pot

Oatmeal in the *Instant Pot* tastes very similar to oatmeal on the stove. Prep time 5 minutes. Cook time 20 minutes. Serves 4.

Ingredients

- 1 c steel cut oats
- 3 c water
- 1 c milk
- 1/4 tsp salt

Instructions:

Combine ingredients in *Instant Pot*. Cook on manual for 20 minutes. Natural release for 10 minutes. Fluff and serve with your favorite toppings. Ours are pumpkin puree, pecans, and pumpkin pie seasonings; or dried pineapple, macadamia nuts, and coconut.

Biscuits and Gravy on the Stove

Occasionally, having a country breakfast like this one is a real treat. Prep time 5 minutes. Cook time 15 minutes. Serves 4.

Ingredients

- 1 lb. package *Jimmy Dean* sage sausage
- OR 1 lb. *Jimmy Dean* regular sausage and ¾ tsp sage
- 3 T flour (Reg or Gluten Free)

- 2 c milk (whole milk tastes better)
- Refrigerator biscuits cooked according to package or make your own favorite biscuit recipe

Instructions:

Cook the sausage in a skillet over medium heat until it is no longer pink 7-8 minutes. Sprinkle the flour over the sausage, and stir until absorbed about 1 minute. Slowly stir in the milk, and cook until thickened about 5 minutes. Season with salt and pepper. Serve over biscuits.

Biscuits and Gravy in the Slow Cooker

The slow cooker gives this dish a nice full flavor. My family loves this recipe cooked this way.

Prep time 15 -20 minutes. Cook time 3 hours. Serves 4.

Ingredients

- 1 lb. package *Jimmy Dean* sage sausage
- OR 1 lb. *Jimmy Dean* regular sausage and ¾ tsp sage
- 3 T flour (Reg or Gluten Free)
- 2 c milk (whole is better)
- 10 refrigerated biscuits cut into halves

Instructions:

Cook the sausage in a skillet over medium heat until it is no longer pink 7-8 minutes. Sprinkle the flour over the sausage, and stir until absorbed about 1 minute. Slowly stir in the milk, and cook until thickened about 5 minutes. Spray slow cooker with cooking spray. Separate each can of dough into 10 biscuits total. Cut biscuits into quarters. Arrange biscuit pieces in slow cooker in bottom, and up the sides. Pour sausage mixture into slow cooker. Place triple layer of towels on top of ingredients. Cover and cook on low setting for 3 hours until biscuits are cooked through. Season with salt and pepper to taste.

Biscuits and Gravy in the Instant Pot

This is very similar to the stove top method.
Prep time 5 minutes. Cook time 15 minutes. Serves 4.

Ingredients

- 1 lb. package *Jimmy Dean* sage sausage
- OR 1 lb. *Jimmy Dean* regular sausage and ¾ tsp sage
- 3 T flour (Reg or Gluten Free)

- 2 c milk (whole is better)
- Refrigerator biscuits OR your favorite homemade biscuit recipe

Instructions:

Turn the *Instant Pot* to Sauté mode. When hot, add a little oil to coat the bottom of the pan, and add the sausage. Cook stirring until meat is no longer pink 7-8 minutes. Sprinkle the flour over the sausage, and stir until absorbed about 1 minute. Slowly stir in the milk, and cook until thickened about 5 minutes. Season with salt and pepper to taste. Serve over biscuits.

Lunch

We love soup with some homemade bread on the side.

- Chicken noodle soup
- French onion soup with chicken
- Tortilla soup

Chicken Noodle Soup on the Stove

I like to make my chicken noodle soup with homemade noodles. The noodles are easy to make and freeze ahead of time. You can substitute egg noodles in a pinch.

Prep time 15 minutes. Cook time 35 minutes. 4-6 servings.

Ingredients

- 1 T vegetable oil
- 1 onion minced
- 3 carrots sliced
- 1 clove garlic minced
- 2 tsp minced fresh thyme

- 2 bay leaves
- 6 cups chicken broth
- 2 cups cooked chicken
- 1 14.5 oz. can peas
- 1 c homemade noodles or egg noodles

Instructions:

Heat oil in Dutch oven until smoking. Turn heat down to low. Add onion and carrots and cook until tender, 5-7 minutes. Add garlic and thyme, and cook for 30 seconds. Add bay leaves, chicken broth, chicken, and peas, and simmer for 20 minutes. Add noodles and cook for 10 more minutes. Remove bay leaves. Serve with fresh homemade dinner rolls.

Chicken Noodle Soup in the Slow Cooker

The slow cooker is my favorite method of cooking soup because it is so flavorful.

Prep time 15 minutes. Cook time 4-6 hours. 4-6 servings.

Ingredients

- 1 T vegetable oil
- 1 onion minced
- 3 carrots sliced
- 1 clove garlic minced
- 2 tsp minced fresh thyme

- 2 bay leaves
- 6 cups chicken broth
- 1 ½ lbs. boneless, skinless, chicken thighs
- ½ c frozen peas
- 1 c homemade noodles or egg noodles

Instructions:

Heat oil in Dutch oven until smoking. Turn heat down to low. Add onion and carrots, and cook until tender 5-7 minutes. Add garlic and thyme, and cook for 30 seconds. Add 1 c Chicken broth, and transfer mixture to slow cooker. Add the rest of the chicken broth and bay leaves. Nestle chicken thighs in the soup. Cook on low 4-6 hours. Cook homemade noodles in boiling water for 10 minutes, or cook egg noodles according to package directions. Remove chicken to cutting board, and let cool enough to touch. Cut chicken into bite sized pieces, and return to slow cooker. Remove bay leaves. Add peas and noodles. Serve with fresh homemade dinner rolls.

Chicken Noodle Soup in the Instant Pot

Using the *Instant Pot* for soup is fast and tastes delicious.
Prep time 15 minutes. Cook time 30 minutes. 4-6 servings.

Ingredients

- 1 T vegetable oil
- 1 onion minced
- 3 carrots sliced
- 1 clove garlic minced
- 2 tsp minced fresh thyme

- 2 bay leaves
- 6 cups chicken broth
- 1 ½ lbs. boneless, skinless, chicken thighs
- ½ c frozen peas
- 1 c homemade noodles or egg noodles

Instructions:

Heat oil in *Instant Pot* on sauté mode. When timer dings, brown chicken thighs on both sides. Remove chicken to a plate. Add more oil to the pot, if needed; cook onions and carrots until tender. Add garlic and thyme, and cook a few seconds. Turn *Instant Pot* off. Add bay leaves, chicken broth, and chicken. Press Manual on the *Instant Pot* and set timer for 20 minutes. When timer dings, do a quick release, and turn *Instant Pot* off. Transfer chicken to cutting board. Press Sauté mode. When soup boils, add noodles and cook for 5-10 minutes. Add peas and cook for 1 minutes. Cut chicken into bite sized pieces and return to soup. Remove bay leaves. Serve with fresh homemade dinner rolls.

Option:

You could use already cooked chicken in the recipe and reduce the cooking time to 4 minutes.

French Onion Soup with Chicken on the Stove

I add chicken to my French onion soup which turns it into a much fuller meal. I also use 3 cheeses on the toast which makes it very cheesy.

Prep time 15 minutes. Cook time 50 minutes. 4-6 servings.

Ingredients

- ¼ c unsalted butter
- 2 T olive oil
- 4 yellow onions sliced
- 1 T brown sugar
- 1 tsp minced thyme
- 1 tsp salt
- 1 tsp pepper
- 5 T flour
- ¾ c apple butter

- ¾ c dry sherry
- ¼ c tamari sauce
- 2 c chicken broth
- 2 c beef broth
- French bread
- shredded Gruyere cheese
- Provolone cheese
- shredded Parmesan cheese
- 1 lb. boneless, skinless, chicken breasts

Instructions:

Mix flour, apple butter, sherry, tamari sauce, and set aside. Melt butter and olive oil in stock pot on medium heat. Add onions and stir until translucent. Do not brown. Add sugar, thyme, salt, and pepper. Cook 15-20 minutes to caramelize the onions. Add the apple butter mixture and the broths. Add the chicken and simmer 30 minutes. Transfer chicken to cutting board and let cool for a bit. Cut the chicken and put it back in the stock pot. Place French bread on cooking sheet. Broil until brown on each side 1-2 minutes. Add Gruyere cheese, Provolone cheese and Parmesan cheese, and broil until melted. Serve soup topped with bread.

French Onion Soup with Chicken Slow Cooker

Prep time 10-15 minutes. Cook time 8-12 hours. 4-6 servings.

Ingredients

- ¼ c unsalted butter melted
- 4 yellow onions sliced
- 1 T brown sugar
- 1 tsp minced thyme
- 1 tsp salt
- 1 tsp pepper
- 5 T flour
- ¾ c apple butter
- ¾ c dry sherry

- ¼ c tamari sauce
- 2 c chicken broth
- 2 c beef broth
- French bread
- shredded Gruyere cheese
- Provolone cheese
- shredded Parmesan cheese
- 1 lb. boneless, skinless, chicken breasts

Instructions:

Add onions, butter, salt, pepper, sugar, and thyme to slow cooker. Mix flour, apple butter, sherry, tamari sauce, and pour over onions. Cover and cook on high 8-12 hours. In second slow cooker; add chicken broth, beef broth, and chicken. Cover and cook on low 4 hours. Transfer chicken to cutting board and let cool for a bit. Cut the chicken and put with the onions, in the first slow cooker. Add the broth to the onions, in the first slow cooker, and stir. Place French bread on cooking sheet. Broil until brown on each side 1-2 minutes. Add Gruyere, Provolone, and Parmesan cheese, and broil until melted. Serve soup topped with bread.

French Onion Soup with Chicken Instant Pot

Chicken breast meat needs the same cooking time as the onions. Prep time 30-40 minutes. Cook time 8 minutes. 4-6 servings.

Ingredients

- ¼ c unsalted butter melted
- 2 T olive oil
- 3 yellow onions sliced
- 1 T brown sugar
- 1 tsp minced thyme
- 1 tsp salt
- 1 tsp pepper
- 5 T flour
- ¾ c apple butter
- ¾ c dry sherry

- ¼ c tamari sauce
- 2 c chicken broth
- 2 c beef broth
- French bread
- shredded Gruyere cheese
- Provolone cheese
- shredded Parmesan cheese
- 1 lb. boneless, skinless, chicken breasts cut into bite sized pieces

Instructions:

Mix flour, apple butter, sherry, and tamari sauce and set aside. Turn *Instant Pot* to Sauté mode. When hot, add oil, and chicken pieces. Brown the chicken 2-3 minutes, then add the butter and onions. Cook until softened but not browned 5-10 minutes. Add sugar, thyme, salt, and pepper. Stir until caramelized 15-20 minutes. Turn off *Instant Pot*. Add chicken pieces, apple butter mixture, chicken broth, and beef broth. Turn *Instant Pot* to Manual and cook for 8 minutes. Manual release for 5 minutes and then quick release. Place French bread on cooking sheet. Broil until brown on each side 1-2 minutes. Add Gruyere, Provolone, and Parmesan cheese, and broil until melted. Serve soup topped with bread.

Tortilla Soup on the Stove

This is a hearty, country version of Tortilla soup. I like to serve it with fresh cornbread.
Prep time 15 minutes. Cook time 30 minutes. 6-8 servings.

Ingredients

- 2 14.5 oz. cans chopped tomatoes
- 1 14.5 oz. can kidney beans
- 1 14.5 oz. can pinto beans
- 1 14.5 oz. can corn
- 2 8 oz. cans tomato sauce
- 2 cloves garlic minced
- 4 cups chicken broth
- 2 T sugar
- 1 T chili powder

- 1 tsp salt
- ½ tsp oregano
- 1 tsp cumin
- ½ c deli salsa
- 1 ½ lb. boneless, skinless chicken thighs

Toppings:

- Tortilla chips, corn chips, cheese, sour cream, chopped avocado, etc.

Instructions:

Pour all ingredients into a Dutch oven. Nestle chicken in the soup. Bring to a boil over medium high heat. Reduce heat to low and simmer 30 minutes. Take out chicken and cut into bite size pieces. Return cut up chicken to soup and serve. You may want to top the soup with Tortilla chips, corn chips, cheese, sour cream, and chopped avocado.

Tortilla Soup in the Slow Cooker

Using the slow cooker for soup is my favorite cooking method. It gives the soup extra flavor. Prep time 15 minutes. Cook time 4 hours. 6-8 servings.

Ingredients

- 2 14.5 oz. cans chopped tomatoes
- 1 14.5 oz. can kidney beans
- 1 14.5 oz. can pinto beans
- 1 14.5 oz. can corn
- 2 8 oz. cans tomato sauce
- 2 cloves garlic minced
- 4 cups chicken broth
- 2 T sugar
- 1 T chili powder
- 1 tsp salt

- ½ tsp oregano
- 1 tsp cumin
- ½ c deli salsa
- 1 1/2 lbs. boneless, skinless, chicken thighs

Toppings:

- Tortilla chips, corn chips, cheese, sour cream, chopped avocado, etc.

Instructions:

Pour all ingredients into a slow cooker and stir to combine. Nestle chicken thighs into soup. Cook on low 4 hours. Transfer chicken thighs to cutting board. Let cool briefly. Cut chicken into bit sized pieces, and return to soup. Serve. You may want to top the soup with Tortilla chips, corn chips, cheese, sour cream, and chopped avocado.

Tortilla Soup in the Instant Pot

Soup in the *Instant Pot* is quicker and more convenient. DO NOT OVERFILL the pot. All ingredients need to fill the pot to 2/3 or less. Prep time 15 minutes. Cook time 20 minutes. 6-8 servings.

Ingredients

- 2 14.5 oz. cans chopped tomatoes
- 1 14.5 oz. can kidney beans
- 1 14.5 oz. can pinto beans
- 1 14.5 oz. can corn
- 2 8 oz. cans tomato sauce
- 2 cloves garlic minced
- ADD AFTER COOKING - 4 cups chicken broth
- 2 T sugar
- 1 T chili powder
- 1 tsp salt
- ½ tsp oregano
- 1 tsp cumin
- ½ c deli salsa
- 1 1/2 lbs. boneless, skinless, chicken thighs
- 1 T oil

Toppings:

- Tortilla chips, corn chips, cheese, sour cream, chopped avocado, etc.

Instructions:

Turn *Instant Pot* to Sauté mode. When hot, add oil, and brown chicken on both sides. Turn *Instant Pot* off. Pour all ingredients into the *Instant Pot* EXCEPT the chicken broth. DO NOT OVERFILL THE INSTANT POT. Nestle chicken thighs into soup. Cook on manual 20 minutes. Turn *Instant Pot* off and slow release for 10 minutes then quick release. Bring the chicken broth to boil on the stove and add to soup. Transfer chicken thighs to cutting board. Let cool briefly. Cut chicken into bit sized pieces and return to soup. Serve. You may want to top the soup with Tortilla chips, corn chips, cheese, sour cream, and chopped avocado.

Dinner

I love having different cooking options for the same meal. I hope it helps you cook more meals at home.

- Baby back ribs
- Cashew chicken
- Cheesy chicken
- Macaroni and cheese
- Penne
- Meatloaf
- Mongolian beef
- Salmon

Baby Back Ribs in the Oven

Ribs cooked slowly in the oven have good texture and flavor. Prep time is 10 minutes and cook time is 3-3 1/2 hours. 6-8 servings.

Ingredients

- 3 T sweet or smoked paprika
- 3 T dark brown sugar
- 1 T salt
- 1 T pepper
- 1 T onion powder
- 1 T garlic powder
- ¼ tsp cayenne pepper
- 6 pounds pork baby back ribs
- 18 oz. BBQ sauce

Instructions:

Mix paprika, sugar, salt, pepper, onion powder, garlic powder, and cayenne pepper in a small bowl. Rub mixture on both sides of the ribs. Preheat oven to 250 degrees. Brush ribs with BBQ sauce. Cover ribs with foil. Bake for 2 hours 30 minutes to 3 hours until tender. Remove from oven. Position oven rack 10 inches from broiling element. Remove foil. Brush ribs with sauce that has dripped onto the pan, and broil for 4 minutes. Turn ribs over and brush sauce on the ribs every 2 minutes broiling for 10-12 more minutes.

Baby Back Ribs in the Slow Cooker

Ribs in the slow cooker are my favorite way of cooking them.
They meat just falls off the bones and the flavor is wonderful.
Prep time is 10 minutes and cook time is 8 ½ -10 ½ hours. 6-8 servings.

Ingredients

- 3 T sweet or smoked paprika
- 3 T dark brown sugar
- 1 T salt
- 1 T pepper
- 1 T onion powder
- 1 T garlic powder
- ¼ tsp cayenne pepper
- 6 pounds pork baby back ribs
- 18 oz. BBQ Sauce

Instructions:

Spray slow cooker insert with cooking spray or line with slow cooker liner. Mix paprika, sugar, salt, pepper, onion powder, garlic powder, and cayenne pepper in a small bowl. Rub on both sides of the ribs. Arrange ribs in the slow cooker upright with the meaty side facing outward. Pour BBQ sauce over ribs, cover, and cook on low 8-10 hours. (If I only have 8 hours to cook these, I usually turn them up to high for the last hour of cooking to make sure the meat falls off the bone). Position oven rack 10 inches from broiling element. Place ribs meaty side down on foil lined baking sheet. Cover with foil to keep warm. Transfer sauce to pan and simmer on stove for 15-20 minutes. Remove foil from ribs and brush ribs with sauce. Broil for 4 minutes. Turn ribs over, brush sauce on the ribs every 2 minutes, broiling for 10-12 more minutes.

Baby Back Ribs in the Instant Pot

Ribs in the *Instant Pot* are a little fattier because the fat doesn't cook off. Prep time is 10 minutes and cook time is 45 minutes after pressure and 15 minutes under the broiler. 3-4 servings.

Ingredients

- 1 1/2 T sweet or smoked paprika
- 1 1/2 T dark brown sugar
- 1 ½ tsp salt
- 1 ½ tsp pepper
- 1 ½ T onion powder

- 1 ½ T garlic powder
- 1/8 tsp cayenne pepper
- 2.5 - 3 pounds pork baby back ribs
- 9 oz. BBQ sauce
- 1 ½ c chicken broth

Instructions:

Cut ribs into sections of 3 ribs and set aside. Mix paprika, sugar, salt, pepper, onion powder, garlic powder, and cayenne pepper in a small bowl. Rub mixture on both sides of the ribs. Place ribs in *Instant Pot*. Pour chicken broth over ribs. Close lid and set to manual for 30 minutes. Natural release for 10 minutes. Quick release the rest of the steam. Position oven rack 10 inches from broiling element. Transfer ribs, meaty side down, to baking sheet and pour BBQ sauce over them. Broil for 4 minutes. Turn ribs over. Brush sauce on the ribs every 2 minutes, broiling for 10-12 more minutes.

Cashew Chicken on the Stove

You can substitute whatever vegetables you like for the onions and water chestnuts in this recipe.

Prep time is 20-30 minutes and cook time is 30 minutes. 4 servings.

Ingredients

- 1 egg white
- 1 T soy sauce + ¼ c soy sauce
- 1 T + 1 tsp cornstarch
- 1 ½ lbs. skinless, boneless, chicken breast cut into chunks
- 1 T dry sherry
- 2 tsp cider vinegar
- 1 tsp sugar

- ½ tsp toasted sesame oil
- ¼ c vegetable oil
- 1 c cashews
- 1 clove garlic minced
- 1-inch ginger peeled and quartered
- 2 green onions sliced
- 1 can (8 oz.) water chestnuts, drained and sliced

Instructions:

Combine egg white, 1 T cornstarch, 1 T soy sauce. Add chicken and toss to coat. Set aside. Combine ¼ c soy sauce, 1 tsp cornstarch, sherry, cider vinegar, sugar, and sesame oil. Set aside. Heat vegetable oil in wok or large frying pan over medium heat. Fry cashews for 1 minute. Remove with a slotted spoon and drain on paper towels. Add chicken and cook until opaque about 5-6 minutes. Remove with a slotted spoon and drain on paper towels. Add ginger, onions, garlic, and water chestnuts and cook for 1 minute. Add sauce and cook until thickened. Remove ginger pieces. Add chicken and cashews. Serve over rice.

Cashew Chicken in the Slow Cooker

The chicken turns out really tender in the slow cooker full of flavor. Prep time is 20-30 minutes and cook time is 4 hours. 4 servings.

Ingredients

- 1 egg white
- 1 T soy sauce + 1/4 c soy sauce
- ¼ c water
- 1 T + 2 T cornstarch
- 1 ½ lbs. skinless, boneless, chicken breast cut into chunks
- 1 T dry sherry
- 2 tsp cider vinegar
- 1 tsp toasted sesame oil

- 1 tsp sugar
- 1-inch ginger peeled and quartered
- 1 clove of garlic minced
- ¼ c vegetable oil
- 1 c cashews
- 2 green onions sliced
- 1 can (8 oz.) water chestnuts, drained, and sliced

Instructions:

Combine egg white, 1 T cornstarch, 1 T soy sauce. Add chicken and toss to coat. Set aside. Combine 1/4 c soy sauce, sherry, cider vinegar, sesame oil, sugar, and garlic. Set aside. Heat vegetable oil in wok or frying pan over medium heat. Add chicken and brown 2-3 minutes. Add chicken to slow cooker. Pour tamari mixture and water over chicken. Add ginger pieces and stir. Cook on low 3 hours. Mix the 2 T cornstarch with ¼ c water and stir into the slow cooker. Add the vegetables. Cook on low an addition hour. Remove ginger pieces and add cashews at the end. Serve over rice.

Cashew Chicken in the Instant Pot

The *Instant Pot* does such a great job of cooking meat and vegetables perfectly. It is more challenging to get the depth of flavor with the *Instant Pot*. Browning the meat helps.

Prep time is 20-30 minutes and cook time is 8 minutes. 4 servings.

Ingredients

- 1 egg white
- 1 T soy sauce + ½ c soy sauce
- 1 T + 2 T cornstarch
- 1 ½ lbs. skinless, boneless, chicken breast cut into chunks
- 1 T dry sherry
- 2 tsp cider vinegar
- 1/2 tsp toasted sesame oil

- 2 tsp sugar
- 1-inch of peeled ginger quartered
- 1 clove of garlic minced
- ¼ c vegetable oil
- 1 c cashews
- 2 green onions sliced
- 1 can (8 oz.) water chestnuts, drained and sliced

Instructions:

Combine egg white, 1 T cornstarch, 1 T soy sauce. Add chicken and toss to coat. Set aside. Combine soy sauce, sherry, cider vinegar, sesame oil, sugar, and garlic. Set aside. Heat vegetable oil in *Instant Pot* in Sauté mode. When the *Instant Pot* dings, heat cashews, green onions, ginger, and water chestnuts for 1-minute stirring constantly. Remove with a slotted spoon and drain on paper towels. Brown chicken 2-3 minutes. Turn *Instant Pot* off. Pour sauce over chicken. Put lid on and cook on manual for 8 minutes high pressure. Quick release. Mix 2 T corn starch and ¼ c water together. Turn *Instant Pot* to sauté mode. Add the corn starch mixture and cook until sauce is thickened. Remove the ginger pieces and add the cashew mixture. Stir to combine and serve over rice.

Cheesy Chicken in the Oven

This is a tasty dish that my family really enjoys.
Prep time 20-30 minutes and cook time is 60 minutes. 4-6 servings.

Ingredients

- 8 oz. sliced mushrooms
- 2 T onion chopped
- 1 clove garlic minced
- 2 T butter
- 2-3 T flour divided
- 2 c chicken broth
- 1 c cream
- ½ tsp salt
- ¼ tsp pepper

- ¼ tsp nutmeg
- ¼ c sherry
- ¼ c sour cream
- 4 boneless, skinless, chicken breasts
- 4 oz. shredded Swiss cheese
- 4 slices Provolone cheese
- 4 oz. Parmesan cheese
- French fried onions (optional)

Instructions:

Preheat oven to 350 degrees. Melt butter in large frying pan over medium heat until hot. Add onions and mushrooms. Cook until soft. Add garlic and stir to combine. Add 2 T flour and stir. Add chicken broth and stir to thicken. Add cream, 1 T flour, salt, pepper, and nutmeg. Heat to thicken further. Take the pan off the heat. Stir in sherry and sour cream. Spray a 13X9 baking pan with cooking spray. Place chicken in baking pan. Cover the chicken with Swiss cheese and Provolone cheese. Add mushroom mixture. At this point, you can put the dish in the fridge and bake later or you can wrap it up with cling wrap and foil, and freeze. If using right away, bake for 50 minutes. Add Parmesan cheese and bake an additional 10 minutes. Serve with rice. Garnish with French fried onions, if desired. If frozen, do not thaw, cook covered with foil for 1 ½ hours. Uncover, sprinkle with Parmesan cheese, and cook an additional 10 minutes.

Cheesy Chicken in the Slow Cooker

Chicken cooked in the slow cooker is very tender.
Prep time is 20-30 minutes and cook time is 4 hours
with an additional 10 minutes under the broiler. 4-6 servings.

Ingredients

- 8 oz. sliced mushrooms
- 2 T onion chopped
- 1 clove garlic minced
- 2 T butter
- 2-3 T flour divided
- 2 c chicken broth
- 1 c cream
- ½ tsp salt
- ¼ tsp pepper

- ¼ tsp nutmeg
- ¼ c sherry
- ¼ c sour cream
- 4 boneless, skinless, chicken breasts
- 4 oz. shredded Swiss cheese
- 4 slices Provolone cheese
- 4 oz. Parmesan cheese
- French fried onions (optional)

Instructions:

Spray slow cooker with cooking spray or use a slow cooker liner. Melt butter in large frying pan over medium heat until hot. Add onions and mushrooms. Cook until soft. Add garlic and stir to combine. Add 2 T flour and stir. Add chicken broth and stir to thicken. Add cream, 1 T flour, salt, pepper, and nutmeg. Heat to thicken further. Take the pan off the heat. Stir in sherry and sour cream. Place chicken in slow cooker. Cover the chicken with Swiss cheese and Provolone cheese. Add mushroom mixture. Cook on low for 4 hours. Add Parmesan cheese and cook an additional 10 minutes. For a crunchy crust, transfer chicken mixture to a 13X9 baking pan, add parmesan cheese and broil until cheese has melted and formed a crust. Serve with rice. Garnish with French fried onions, if desired.

Cheesy Chicken in the Instant Pot

It's tough to cook more than 2 chicken breasts in the *Instant Pot*.
Prep time is 20-30 minutes. Cook time is 13 minutes. 2-3 servings.

Ingredients

- 8 oz. sliced mushrooms
- 2 T onion chopped
- 1 clove garlic minced
- 2 T butter
- 2-3 T flour divided
- 2 c chicken broth
- 1 c cream
- ½ tsp salt
- ¼ tsp pepper

- ¼ tsp nutmeg
- ¼ c sherry
- ¼ c sour cream
- 2 boneless, skinless, chicken breasts
- 2 oz. shredded Swiss cheese
- 2 slices Provolone cheese
- 2 oz. Parmesan cheese
- French fried onions (optional)

Instructions:

Turn *Instant Pot* to sauté mode. When hot, add butter. Once the butter has melted, add onions, and mushrooms. Cook until soft, about 5 minutes. Add garlic and stir to combine. Add 2 T flour and stir. Add chicken broth and stir to thicken. Add salt, pepper, and nutmeg. Stir to combine. Add sherry. Place trivet in the *Instant Pot* and place chicken on trivet. Put lid on and cook for 8 minutes on manual. Allow natural release for 5 minutes and quick release the rest of the steam. Turn *Instant Pot* off. Remove chicken and trivet. Turn sauté mode back on. Add cream and 1 T flour and stir until thickened. Add sour cream and turn off *Instant Pot*. Grease a 13X9 baking pan. Add chicken, cover with Swiss cheese and Provolone cheese. Cover with mushroom mixture. Top with Parmesan cheese. Broil in the oven until cheese has melted and formed a crunchy crust. Serve with rice. Garnish with French fried onions, if desired.

Macaroni and Cheese in the Oven

I like to add bacon to my macaroni and cheese to give it depth and texture. You can also add hot dogs or kielbasa to add more protein and flavor.

Prep time is 30 minutes and cook time is 40 minutes. 6-8 servings.

Ingredients

- 1 pkg. (16 oz.) elbow macaroni
- 6 T unsalted butter
- 6 T flour
- 1 clove garlic minced
- ¼ tsp dried thyme
- ¼ tsp cayenne pepper
- 1 tsp salt
- 1/8 tsp pepper
- 1 pinch nutmeg

- 2 ¼ c chicken broth
- 3 ½ c whole milk
- 1 lb. Colby Jack cheese
- 8 oz. extra sharp Cheddar cheese
- 8 oz. Gruyere cheese
- 1 tsp Dijon mustard
- ¾ cup bacon bits or 12 slices of bacon cooked and crumbled
- Sliced hot dog or kielbasa (optional)

Instructions:

Cook macaroni according to package directions. While macaroni is cooking, melt butter in stock pot. Stir in garlic, thyme, salt, pepper, cayenne pepper, and nutmeg. Cook for 15 seconds stirring constantly. Add flour and cook for 30 seconds stirring constantly. Slowly whisk in chicken broth and milk. Bring to a simmer and cook for 15 minutes. Take pan off the heat. Add cheese and stir until melted. Add Dijon mustard and stir. Add macaroni and bacon. Stir to combine. Pour into whatever pan or pans you are using. If using immediately, bake at 400 degrees, covered with foil for 20 minutes. Remove foil and bake for 20 more minutes until hot and bubbling.

Make Ahead Options:

Instead of baking right away, you can refrigerate and bake it later. Increase baking time to 25 minutes under foil and 20 minutes without foil. You can also freeze for up to 2 months. You can divide the mixture among foil loaf pans, square pans, or lasagna pans depending on the portions you want.

Macaroni and Cheese in the Slow Cooker

Macaroni and cheese in the slow cooker is easy and tastes delicious. Prep time 20-30 minutes. Cook time is 1 ½ - 3 hours. 6-8 servings.

Ingredients

- 1 pkg. (16 oz.) elbow macaroni
- 1 clove garlic minced
- ¼ tsp dried thyme
- Pinch cayenne pepper
- 1/2 tsp salt
- 1/4 tsp pepper
- 1 pinch nutmeg
- 2 (12 oz.) cans evaporated milk
- 2 (11 oz.) cans Cheddar cheese soup

- 2 ½ cups hot water
- 8 oz. Gruyere Cheese
- 8 oz. Colby Jack cheese, Monterey Jack or Mexican blend cheese
- 8 oz. extra sharp Cheddar cheese
- 1 tsp Dijon mustard
- ¾ cup bacon bits or 12 slices of bacon cooked and crumbled

Instructions:

Make a foil collar measuring 16 inches by 4 inches and has six layers. Place collar in the backside of the slow cooker. Add a slow cooker liner, if using. Bring milk, soup, water, garlic thyme, cayenne pepper, salt, pepper, and nutmeg to simmer in large pot. Whisk in cheese until melted. Stir in macaroni. Transfer to slow cooker. Cover and cook for 1-1 1/2 hours on high or 2-3 hours on low. Stir to combine. Add Dijon mustard and stir. Top with bacon and serve.

Macaroni and Cheese in the Instant Pot

This is not your everyday macaroni and cheese. It is very cheesy.
My family goes back for seconds when I make it.
Prep time 20 minutes. Cook time 2 minutes plus natural release. 6-8 servings.

Ingredients

- 1 pkg. (16 oz.) elbow macaroni
- 4 cups water
- 6 T butter
- 6 T flour
- 1 clove garlic minced
- ¼ tsp dried thyme
- ¼ tsp cayenne pepper
- 1 tsp salt
- 1/8 tsp pepper
- 1 pinch nutmeg
- 2 ¼ c chicken broth
- 3 ½ c whole milk
- 16 oz. Colby Jack cheese
- 8 oz. extra sharp Cheddar cheese
- 8 oz. Gruyere cheese
- 1 tsp Dijon mustard
- ¾ cup bacon bits or 12 slices of bacon cooked and crumbled

Instructions:

Press Sauté on the *Instant Pot* and add butter. When butter has melted, add garlic, thyme, cayenne pepper, salt, pepper, nutmeg, and cook for 15 seconds stirring constantly. Add flour and cook for 30 seconds stirring constantly. Wisk in chicken broth and whole milk. Bring to a simmer. Turn *Instant Pot* off. Add macaroni and cook on manual for 2 minutes. Natural release. Turn *Instant Pot* off. Stir in cheese. Put lid back on and allow the cheese to melt. Take the lid off, add milk, if needed, and Dijon mustard. Top with bacon and serve.

Baked Penne in the Oven

Easier than lasagna and just as tasty.

Prep time 20-30 minutes. Cook time 60-70 minutes. 6-8 servings.

Ingredients

- 12 oz. whole milk ricotta cheese (optional)
- 2 T olive oil
- ½ tsp salt
- ½ tsp pepper
- 12 oz. shredded Mozzarella cheese
- 3 oz. Parmesan cheese
- 1 ½ lbs. penne pasta
- 1 ½ c pasta cooking water
- 1 24 oz. jar marinara sauce
- 1 pkg. *Jimmy Dean* Sage Sausage or 1 pkg. *Jimmy Dean* regular sausage plus ½ tsp sage
- ¼ c bacon crumbles or 4 slices of bacon cooked and crumbled

Instructions:

Preheat oven to 400 degrees. Cook penne according to package directions reserving 1 ½ cups of pasta cooking water. In a separate bowl, toss the Mozzarella cheese and Parmesan cheese together. Cook the *Jimmy Dean* sausage in a skillet until browned. Drain the sausage on a paper towel. Put the sausage back into the skillet. Add the bacon and marinara sauce, pasta cooking water, salt, pepper, and olive oil. Add the cooked penne and stir. In whatever pan or pans you are using, (see below) pour half the sausage mixture into the pan(s), drop large spoonsful of ricotta cheese over the sausage layer, if using, then pour remaining sausage mixture on top the ricotta layer. Sprinkle the top with the blended cheese mixture. If using right away, cover dish with foil and bake for 30-40 minutes. Remove foil and bake for 25-30 minutes until cheese is beginning to brown and sauce is bubbling.

You can use a 13X9X2 pan or substitute 2 8X8 pans or 3 loaf pans for this recipe.

Make Ahead Option:

You can bake the dish right away or you can freeze for a couple of months. If frozen, thaw in the fridge for 24 hours, and then bake at 400 degrees, covered in foil, for 25 minutes. Uncover and bake an additional 20 minutes.

Penne in the Slow Cooker

I love meals I can put in the slow cooker and forget about until dinner time.
Prep time 10-15 minutes. Cook time 2-3 hours. 6-8 servings.

Ingredients

- 8 oz. whole milk ricotta cheese (optional)
- 8 oz. Italian blend cheese
- 8 oz. penne pasta
- 1 jar marinara sauce
- 1 pkg. *Jimmy Dean* sage sausage or 1 pkg. *Jimmy Dean* regular sausage and ½ tsp sage
- 1/3 c bacon crumbles or 5 slices of bacon cooked and crumbled
- 1 tsp. salt
- ½ tsp. pepper

Instructions:

Make a foil collar measuring 16 inches by 4 inches and has six layers. Place collar on the backside of the slow cooker. Add a liner if using. Microwave *Jimmy Dean* sausage until browned, stirring often, about 5 minutes. Drain. Add bacon, marinara sauce, 1 tsp. salt and ½ tsp. pepper, and stir to combine. Place penne in slow cooker. Cover pasta with sausage mixture. Add 1 ½ cups of water and stir. Cover and cook for 2-3 hours on high. Top with spoonsful of ricotta cheese, if using, and cover with Italian cheese blend. Put lid back on and cook on high for 10 minutes until cheese is melted. Serve with garlic bread and a Caesar salad.

Penne in the Instant Pot

Pasta in the *Instant Pot* is soft and gooey with perfectly melted cheese. Prep time 10-15 minutes. Cook time 4 minutes. 3-4 servings.

Ingredients

- 8 oz. whole milk ricotta cheese (optional)
- 8 oz. Italian blend cheese
- 8 oz. penne pasta
- 1 jar marinara sauce
- 1 pkg. *Jimmy Dean* sage sausage or 1 pkg. *Jimmy Dean* regular sausage and ½ tsp sage
- ¼ c bacon crumbles or 4 slices of bacon cooked and crumbled

Instructions:

Turn *Instant Pot* on to sauté mode. When hot, add the *Jimmy Dean* sausage and cook until browned. Turn *Instant Pot* off. Add the bacon and stir. Add the marinara sauce, 1 cup of water, and the penne pasta. Select manual and cook at high pressure for 4 minutes. Natural release for 10 minutes. Add the ricotta cheese by spoonsful, if using, and the Italian cheese blend and put the lid back on. Let it set for 5 minutes. Serve with garlic bread and salad.

Meatloaf in the Oven

Blue cheese compliments beef well. This is a simple but tasty meatloaf. Prep time is 10 minutes and cook time is 45-60 minutes. 4 servings.

Ingredients

- 1 lb. ground beef
- 1 4 oz. pkg. blue cheese crumbles
- ½ tsp salt
- ¼ tsp pepper
- ¾ tsp rubbed sage
- ½ c quick oats
- ¼ cup milk
- 1 egg

Instructions:

Spray 8X4 loaf pan with cooking spray. Mix all ingredients together and form into a loaf. Place in loaf pan. Bake in 350-degree oven for 45-60 minutes. Serve with mashed potatoes and green beans.

Meatloaf in the Slow Cooker

The slow cooker version isn't really a loaf but still tastes good.
Prep time is 10 minutes and cook time is 4-8 hours. 4 servings.

Ingredients

- 1 lb. ground beef
- 1 4 oz. pkg. blue cheese crumbles
- ½ tsp salt
- ¼ tsp pepper
- ¾ tsp rubbed sage
- ½ c quick oats
- ¼ cup milk
- 1 egg

Instructions:

Spray slow cooker with cooking spray, or line slow cooker. Mix all ingredients together and spread in slow cooker. Cook on low 6-8 hours or on high 4 hours. Serve with mashed potatoes and green beans.

Meatloaf in the Instant Pot

You may want to finish the meatloaf in the oven to get a crispy outside. Prep time is 10 minutes and cook time is 25 minutes. 4 servings.

Ingredients

- 1 lb. ground beef
- 1 4 oz. pkg. blue cheese crumbles
- ½ tsp salt
- ¼ tsp pepper
- ¾ tsp rubbed sage
- ½ c quick oats
- ¼ cup milk
- 1 egg

Instructions:

Mix all ingredients together and form into a loaf that will fit in your *Instant Pot*. Put 1 ½ cups of water in the *Instant Pot* and the trivet. Make a foil sling wide enough to hold the meatloaf. Place sling in the *Instant Pot* and place meatloaf on sling. Place lid on pot and set to manual for 25 minutes. When the pot beeps, do a quick release. Remove lid and turn *Instant Pot* off. You may want to transfer meatloaf to the oven and broil for a couple of minutes to brown the top. Remove from oven, when browned. Serve with mashed potatoes and green beans.

Mongolian Beef on the Stove

This version has added flavor because of the extra onions.
Prep time is 20-30 minutes and cook time is 20-30 minutes.
4-6 servings.

Ingredients

- 1 T olive oil
- 1 ½ lbs. flank steak cut into 1-inch strips
- 2 c sliced onions
- ¾ c dark brown sugar
- ½ c tamari sauce
- ½ tsp toasted sesame oil
- ½ c water
- 1 T grated ginger
- 5 cloves garlic minced
- 2 T cornstarch
- 2 green onions
- cooked rice

Instructions:

Mix together brown sugar, tamari sauce, water, ginger, garlic, and corn starch. Set aside. Heat ½ T of the olive oil in skillet or wok. Cook the onions until tender about 5-10 minutes. Remove onions from pan. Add another ½ T olive oil. Cook the beef until it is no longer pink. Stir in the sauce and cook until thickened. Add the onions. Top with the green part of the green onions. Serve with rice.

Mongolian Beef in the Slow Cooker

The slow cooker version is easy and full of flavor.
Prep time is 20-30 minutes and cook time is 4-5 hours. 6-8 servings.

Ingredients

- 1 ½ lbs. flank steak cut into 6 portions
- 2 c sliced onions
- ¾ c dark brown sugar
- ½ c tamari sauce
- ¼ tsp toasted sesame oil
- ½ c water

- 1 T grated ginger
- 4 cloves garlic minced
- 2 T cornstarch
- 2 green onions
- cooked rice

Instructions:

Spray insert with cooking spray or line with slow cooker liner. Place steak and onions in slow cooker. Mix together brown sugar, tamari sauce, toasted sesame oil, water, ginger, and garlic. Pour over steak and onions. Cook on low for 8-10 hours or high for 4-5 hours. Mix cornstarch with ¼ c water and stir into the slow cooker. Cook on High for 10-15 minutes until it thickens. Top with the green part of the green onions. Serve with rice.

Mongolian Beef in the Instant Pot

This version has added flavor because of the extra onions.
Prep time is 20-30 minutes. Cook time is 12 minutes. Serves 3-4.

Ingredients

- 1 T olive oil
- 1 ½ lbs. flank steak cut into 1-inch strips
- 2 c sliced onions
- ¾ c dark brown sugar
- ½ c tamari sauce
- ½ c water

- ½ tsp toasted sesame oil
- 1 T grated ginger
- 5 cloves garlic minced
- 2 T cornstarch
- 2 green onions
- cooked white rice

Instructions:

Turn *Instant Pot* on sauté mode. Mix brown sugar, sesame oil, tamari sauce, and water together. Set aside. When *Instant Pot* is hot, add ½ T olive oil, and flank steak. Brown steak 3-5 minutes per side. Remove steak. Add ½ T olive oil. Sauté onions until tender 3-5 minutes. Add garlic and ginger and stir for a few seconds. Add sauce and steak. Turn off *Instant Pot*. Press Manual and cook for 12 minutes. Do a quick release. Mix cornstarch with ¼ c water. Turn *Instant Pot* on sauté mode. Add cornstarch and water mixture stirring constantly until sauce is boiling and has thickened. Top with the green part of the green onions. Serve with rice.

Salmon on the Stove

I'm not a huge fish lover and so my fish has to have a sauce that hides the flavor of the fish.

Prep time is 10 minutes and cook time is 15 minutes. 4 servings.

Ingredients

- 4 skinless salmon fillets
- salt and pepper
- 1 tsp oil
- ¼ c orange juice

- 2 T balsamic vinegar
- 2 T honey
- 1 sprig rosemary

Instructions:

Pat the salmon dry with paper towel. Salt and pepper the salmon on both sides. Heat oil in frying pan over medium heat. Fry salmon on both sides until well browned about 5 minutes each side. Transfer fish to plate and cover with foil. Add orange juice, balsamic vinegar, honey, and rosemary to frying pan. Bring to a simmer and cook until a syrupy glaze. Remove rosemary sprig. Serve salmon with glaze.

Salmon in the Slow Cooker

This is probably the most tender salmon I've ever had.
Prep time is 10 minutes and cook time is 1 ½ hours.
4 servings.

Ingredients

- 4 skinless salmon fillets
- Salt and pepper
- ¼ c orange juice

- 2 T balsamic vinegar
- 2 T honey
- 1 sprig rosemary

Instructions:

Pat the salmon dry with paper towel. Salt and pepper the salmon on both sides. Lay a long sheet of foil on counter. Place fish in center of foil. In a separate bowl, mix orange juice, balsamic vinegar, and honey. Pour over fish. Lay the rosemary sprig over the fish. Fold foil over and crimp edges to enclose the packet. Place packet in slow cooker and cook on low 1 ½ hours until fish is 140 degrees. Remove spring of rosemary and serve.

Salmon in the Instant Pot

Salmon in the *Instant Pot* comes out perfect and flaky.
Prep time is 10 minutes. Cook time is 6 minutes. Servings 3-4.

Ingredients

- 3-4 skinless salmon fillets
- Salt and pepper
- 1 c water
- ¼ c orange juice
- 2 T balsamic vinegar
- 2 T honey
- 1 sprig rosemary

Instructions:

Pat the salmon dry with paper towel. Salt and pepper the salmon on both sides. Place 1 c of water in *Instant Pot*. Place trivet in *Instant Pot* and lay the salmon on the trivet. Put lid on *Instant Pot* and cook on manual for 6 minutes. Do a quick release. Take salmon out and cover with foil. Take trivet out and wipe out the *Instant Pot* with paper towel. Turn *Instant Pot* to sauté mode. Add orange juice, balsamic vinegar, honey, and rosemary. Cook until a syrupy glaze. Remove rosemary and serve salmon with glaze.

Side Dishes

I love doing side dishes in the slow cooker or *Instant Pot*. It means I can do more than canned vegetables, and more things at once.

- Carrots
- Red potatoes
- Green beans

Carrots in the Oven

The bacon compliments the carrots beautifully.
Prep time 10 minutes. Cook time 40 minutes. 4 servings.

Ingredients

- 1 – 1 ½ pounds carrots sliced
- olive oil
- ½ c bacon bits
- ¼ c maple syrup
- ½ tsp salt
- ¼ tsp pepper
- pinch cayenne pepper

Instructions:

Toss carrots with olive oil and place in an 8X8 baking pan. Bake at 400 degrees for 40 minutes. Stir together maple syrup, salt, pepper, and cayenne. Pour over carrots and stir. Top with bacon bits. Cook in the oven 10 more minutes.

Carrots in the Slow Cooker

Be sure to use sliced carrots and not baby carrots.

Prep time 10 minutes. Cook time 4 hours. 4-6 servings.

Ingredients

- 1 – 1 ½ pounds carrots sliced
- ¼ c maple syrup
- ½ tsp salt
- ¼ tsp pepper
- pinch cayenne pepper
- ½ c bacon bits

Instructions:

Line slow cooker with liner or spray slow cooker with cooking spray. Put carrots in slow cooker. Stir together maple syrup, salt, pepper, and cayenne. Pour over carrots and stir. Cook in the slow cooker for 4 hours on low. Add bacon bits and serve.

Carrots in the Instant Pot

This method is fast and easy.
Prep time 10 minutes. Cook time 4 minutes. 4 servings.

Ingredients

- 1 – 1 ½ pounds carrots sliced
- 1 c water
- 1 T butter
- ¼ c maple syrup

- ½ tsp salt
- ¼ tsp pepper
- pinch cayenne pepper
- ½ c bacon bits

Instructions:

Place water in *Instant Pot*. Place carrots in a steam basket and place on a trivet in the *Instant Pot*. Close lid. Select "steam" and cook for 4 minutes. Do a quick release. Turn off *Instant Pot*. Pull the steam basket and trivet out of the *Instant Pot*. Drain water from the pot. Put the pot back and turn on sauté mode. Add 1 T butter, maple syrup, salt, pepper, cayenne, and bacon bits. Add the carrots and sauté until liquid is absorbed. Serve immediately.

Red Potatoes in the Oven

These are a great side dish. You can re-heat leftovers for breakfast and add scrambled eggs to them. Prep time 10 minutes. Cook time 45 minutes. 4 servings.

Ingredients

- 1 lb. red potatoes quartered
- 2 T Olive Oil

Optional Seasonings:

- salt, pepper, garlic, rosemary, parsley, ranch seasonings

Optional Toppings:

- Cheddar cheese, bacon, sour cream, chives

Instructions:

Put potatoes on a foil lined baking sheet. Coat with olive oil and top with seasonings. Bake at 425 degrees uncovered for 40-45 minutes turning halfway through the baking time. If you are going to top with cheese and bacon, add that during the last 10 minutes of the baking time. You may want to serve with sour cream and chives.

Red Potatoes in the Slow Cooker

This is my favorite way of cooking these potatoes.

I love to re-heat the leftovers for breakfast and scramble an egg to put on top. So delicious.

Prep time 10 minutes. Cook time 3-4 hours. 4 servings.

Ingredients

- 2 lb. red potatoes quartered
- 3 T Ranch Seasoning
- 8 oz. Cheddar cheese
- 4 oz. bacon bits

Instructions:

Line slow cooker with foil leaving enough to cover the potatoes. Layer 1/3 of the potatoes, 1 T ranch seasonings, 1/3 cheese, and 1/3 of bacon. Repeat layers until you have 3 layers. Cover with foil and lid. Cook on low 5-6 hours or high 3-4 hours.

Red Potatoes in the Instant Pot

If you like soft potatoes and gooey cheese, this is the dish for you.
Prep time is 10-15 minutes. Cook time is 30 minutes.
3-4 servings.

Ingredients

- 1 lb. red potatoes quartered
- 2 T Butter
- 1/4 c chicken broth
- ¼ c Ranch dressing
- 4 oz. Cheddar cheese
- 2 oz. bacon bits

Instructions:

Melt butter in *Instant Pot* on sauté mode. Add potatoes and fry for 7-8 minutes until crisp. Turn *Instant Pot* off. Add chicken broth. Set to manual for 8 minutes with the steam valve closed. Do a natural release. Remove lid. Add Ranch dressing, cheese and bacon. Put lid back on for 5 minutes. Serve.

Green Beans on the Stove

These green beans are soft and full of flavor.

Prep time 10-15 minutes. Cook time 20 minutes.

1 pound of green beans serves 3-4. 2 pounds would serve 6-8.

Ingredients

- 1 or 2 lbs. green beans trimmed
- 1 or 2 cups chicken broth
- ½ tsp salt
- ¼ tsp pepper

- 1 ham hock or shank
- bacon bits
- freshly grated Parmesan

Instructions:

Put green beans in 12-inch frying pan. Add salt and pepper and stir. Add chicken broth and ham shank. Bring to a simmer. Cover and simmer for 20 minutes. Use a slotted spoon to remove green beans. Garnish with bacon bits and freshly grated Parmesan.

Green Beans in the Slow Cooker

These green beans are soft and full of flavor.

Prep time 10-15 minutes. Cook time 3 hours.

1 pound of green beans serves 3-4.

2 pounds would serve 6-8.

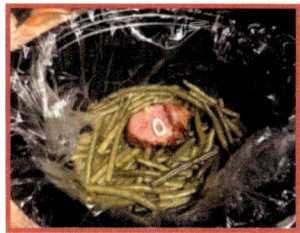

Ingredients

- 1 or 2 lbs. green beans trimmed
- 1 or 2 cups chicken broth
- ½ tsp salt
- ¼ tsp pepper
- 1 ham hock or shank
- bacon bits
- freshly grated Parmesan

Instructions:

Line slow cooker with liner. Put green beans in slow cooker. Add salt and pepper and stir. Add ham shank. Pour chicken broth over green beans. Cook in the slow cooker for 3 hours on high. Use a slotted spoon to remove green beans. Garnish with bacon bits and freshly grated Parmesan.

Green Beans in the Instant Pot

These green beans are soft and full of flavor.

Prep time 10-15 minutes. Cook time 4 minutes.

1 pound of green beans serves 3-4. 2 pounds would serve 6-8.

Ingredients

- 1 lb. green beans trimmed
- 1 c. chicken broth
- ½ tsp salt
- ¼ tsp pepper

- 1 ham hock or shank
- bacon bits
- freshly grated Parmesan

Instructions:

Put green beans in *Instant Pot*. Add salt and pepper and stir. Add ham shank. Pour chicken broth over green beans. Turn *Instant Pot* on to manual and cook for 4 minutes. Do a quick release. Use a slotted spoon to remove green beans. Garnish with bacon bits and freshly grated Parmesan.

Dessert

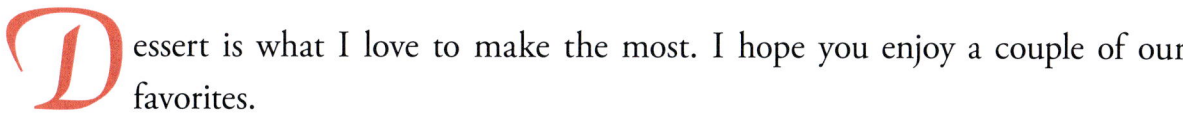essert is what I love to make the most. I hope you enjoy a couple of our favorites.

- Tropical cake
- Cheesecake

Tropical Cake in the Oven

This tea cake has such wonderful tastes and textures.
Prep time 15-20 minutes.
Cook time 40-45 minutes. Serves 6-8.

Ingredients
- ½ cup unsalted butter
- 1 ¼ c flour
- 1 tsp baking powder
- ½ tsp baking soda
- ½ tsp salt
- ½ tsp ground cinnamon
- ½ tsp nutmeg
- ½ c packed dark brown sugar
- 2 large eggs
- 1 tsp vanilla
- ½ c grated carrots
- ½ c crushed pineapple drained
- ¼ c toasted shredded sweetened coconut
- ½ c toasted macadamia nuts

Frosting:
- 8 ounces cream cheese
- 1 cup confectioners' sugar
- ½ tsp vanilla
- 1 T coconut rum
- shredded sweetened coconut

Instructions:
Preheat oven to 350 degrees. Butter and dust with flour a 9X5 loaf pan. Whisk flour, baking powder, baking soda, salt cinnamon, and nutmeg together. In a large bowl, beat butter and brown sugar until fluffy 3-5 minutes. Add eggs and vanilla and mix well. Add flour mixture, carrots, pineapple, coconut, and macadamia nuts. Stir to combine. Transfer batter to loaf pan. Bake for 40-45 minutes until inserted toothpick comes out clean. Turn out cake on wire rack and cool completely. Once cooled, mix frosting ingredients together and frost the cake. Top with coconut.

Tropical Cake in the Slow Cooker

You wouldn't think that cake done in the slow cooker would be so good.

Prep time 15-20 minutes.

Cook time 2 hours. Serves 6-8.

Ingredients

- ½ cup unsalted butter
- 1 ¼ c flour
- 1 tsp baking powder
- ½ tsp baking soda
- ½ tsp salt
- ½ tsp ground cinnamon
- ½ tsp nutmeg
- ½ c packed dark brown sugar
- 2 large eggs
- 1 tsp vanilla
- ½ c grated carrots

- ½ c crushed pineapple drained
- ¼ c toasted shredded sweetened coconut
- ½ c toasted macadamia nuts

Frosting:

- 8 ounces cream cheese
- 1 cup confectioners' sugar
- ½ tsp vanilla
- 1 T coconut rum
- shredded sweetened coconut

Instructions:

Put a wire rack or trivet in the slow cooker. Butter and dust with flour an 8X4 loaf pan. Whisk flour, baking powder, baking soda, salt cinnamon, and nutmeg together. In a large bowl, beat butter and brown sugar until fluffy 3-5 minutes. Add eggs and vanilla, then stir to combine. Add flour mixture, carrots, pineapple, coconut, and macadamia nuts mixing it into the batter. Transfer batter to loaf pan. Place pan in slow cooker. Tent pan with foil. Cover and cook on high 2 hours. Check for doneness with a toothpick. Leave foil off and continue cooking until toothpick comes out clean. Place a paper towel over the slow cooker and place the lid back on. When cake is done, cool on wire rack until cold. Once cooled, mix frosting ingredients together and frost the cake. Top with coconut.

Tropical Cake in the Instant Pot

This is quick and easy and small enough to enjoy with your family.

Prep time 15-20 minutes. Cook time 55 minutes plus a natural release. Serves 3-4.

Ingredients

- ½ cup unsalted butter
- 1 ¼ c flour
- 1 tsp baking powder
- ½ tsp baking soda
- ½ tsp salt
- ½ tsp ground cinnamon
- ½ tsp nutmeg
- ½ c packed dark brown sugar
- 2 large eggs
- 1 tsp vanilla
- ½ c grated carrots

- ½ c crushed pineapple drained
- ¼ c toasted shredded sweetened coconut
- ½ c toasted macadamia nuts

Frosting:

- 8 ounces cream cheese
- 1 cup confectioners' sugar
- ½ tsp vanilla
- 1 T coconut rum
- shredded sweetened coconut

Instructions:

Put a trivet and 1 c water in the *Instant Pot*. Butter and dust with flour a 5-inch loaf pan or a 7-inch spring form pan. Whisk flour, baking powder, baking soda, salt cinnamon, and nutmeg together. In a large bowl, beat butter and brown sugar until fluffy 3-5 minutes. Add eggs and vanilla and stir to combine. Add flour mixture in 3 batches, stirring after each addition. Stir in carrots, pineapple, coconut, and macadamia nuts. Transfer batter to loaf pan. Cover the pan with a paper towel and aluminum foil. Make a foil sling. Place pan of cake on sling and lower into the *Instant Pot*. Place lid on *Instant Pot* and set for manual mode for 55 minutes. Let the cake cool on wire rack until cold. Mix frosting ingredients together and frost the cake. Top with coconut.

Cheesecake in the Oven

This cheesecake is full of unexpected ingredients.
Folks who don't normally like cheesecake, love this cheesecake.
Prep time 15-20 minutes. Cook time 60 minutes. Serves 10-12.

Ingredients

- 1 ½ cups chocolate wafer cookie crumbs
- 3 T sugar
- ¼ c butter melted
- 4 (8 oz.) pkg. cream cheese
- 3 large eggs
- 1 c sugar
- 1 tsp vanilla
- 1 (14 oz.) pkg. flaked sweetened coconut
- 1 (11.5 oz.) pkg. semi-sweet chocolate chips
- ½ c macadamia nuts chopped and toasted

Topping:

- 8 oz. bittersweet chocolate chopped fine
- 1 ¼ c heavy cream
- macadamia nuts chopped and toasted

Instructions:

Stir together chocolate wafer crumbs, sugar, and melted butter. Press mixture in the bottom of a 10-inch springform pan. Bake at 350 degrees for 8 minutes. Cool. Beat cream cheese, eggs, vanilla, and sugar at medium speed until fluffy. Stir in coconut, chocolate chips, and macadamia nuts. Pour batter into cooled crust. Bake at 350 degrees for 1 hour. Cool on wire rack completely. Cheesecake can be frozen for up to a month at this point. Thaw in the fridge for 2 days then finish the topping and serve.

For the topping:

Place chocolate in heatproof bowl. Bring cream to boil over medium heat, pour over chocolate coating completely. Let sit for 10 minutes. Stir chocolate until combined. Let sit for 15 more minutes at room temperature. Pour over cheesecake. Garnish with more chopped and toasted macadamia nuts, if desired.

Cheesecake in the Slow Cooker

If you are worried about your cheesecake falling or cracking, the slow cooker is a better way to avoid those pitfalls. Prep time 20-30 minutes. Cook time 2 hours. Serves 6-8.

Ingredients

- ¾ cup chocolate wafer cookie crumbs regular or gluten free
- 1 ½ T sugar
- 2 T butter melted
- 2 (8 oz.) pkg. cream cheese
- 1 large egg and 1 large egg yolk
- ½ c sugar
- ½ tsp vanilla
- 7 oz. flaked sweetened coconut

- 6 oz. semi-sweet chocolate chips
- ¼ c macadamia nuts chopped and toasted

Topping:

- 4 oz. bittersweet chocolate chopped fine
- ½ c plus 2 T heavy cream
- macadamia nuts chopped and toasted

Instructions:

Fill slow cooker with ½ inch of water. Position wire rack in the bottom. Stir together chocolate wafer crumbs, sugar, and melted butter. Press mixture in the bottom of a 7-inch springform pan. Bake at 350 degrees for 8 minutes. Cool. Beat cream cheese, eggs, vanilla, and sugar at medium speed until fluffy. Stir in coconut, chocolate chips, and macadamia nuts. Pour batter into cooled crust. Set cheesecake in slow cooker with a triple layer of paper towels and the lid. Turn slow cooker to high and cook for 2 hours without removing lid. Turn off slow cooker and let stand for one hour. Remove lid and paper towels and transfer cheesecake to wire rack and cool another hour. Cover cheesecake with plastic wrap and chill in fridge for 4 hours. For the topping, place chocolate in heatproof bowl. Bring cream to boil over medium heat, pour over chocolate coating completely. Let sit for 10 minutes. Stir chocolate until combined. Let sit for 15 more minutes at room temperature. Pour over cheesecake. Garnish with more chopped and toasted macadamia nuts, if desired.

Cheesecake in the Instant Pot

The nice thing about the *Instant Pot* is that you can make a great dessert in a smaller portion.

Prep time 20-30 minutes. Cook time 40 minutes plus natural release. Serves 6-8.

Ingredients

- ¾ cups chocolate wafer cookie crumbs regular or gluten free
- 1 ½ T sugar
- 2 T butter melted
- 2 (8 oz.) pkg. cream cheese
- 1 large egg and 1 large egg yolk
- 1/2 c sugar
- ½ tsp vanilla
- 7 oz. flaked sweetened coconut

- 6 oz. semi-sweet chocolate chips
- ¼ c macadamia nuts chopped and toasted

Topping:

- 4 oz. bittersweet chocolate chopped fine
- ½ c plus 2 T heavy cream
- macadamia nuts chopped and toasted

Instructions:

Wrap bottom of 7-inch springform pan in foil and spray inside with cooking spray. Pour 1 ½ c water in *Instant Pot* and place trivet in *Instant Pot*. Stir together chocolate wafer crumbs, sugar, and melted butter. Press mixture in the bottom of a 7-inch springform pan. Bake at 350 degrees for 8 minutes. Cool. Beat cream cheese, eggs, vanilla, and sugar at medium speed until fluffy. Stir in coconut, chocolate chips, and macadamia nuts. Pour batter into cooled crust. Cover pan with foil. May a foil sling by folding a 20-inch piece of foil in half lengthwise 2 times. Using the sling, place the cheesecake in the *Instant Pot*. Fold down foil sling so you can place the lid on the pot. Cook on manual for 40 minutes. When pot beeps, turn off, and allow pressure to release naturally for 10 minutes and then do a quick release. Carefully, remove cheesecake with sling and allow to cool completely on wire rack for about an hour. Cover cheesecake with plastic wrap and chill in fridge for 8 hours or overnight. For the topping, place chocolate in heatproof bowl. Bring cream to boil over medium heat, pour over chocolate coating completely. Let sit for 10 minutes. Stir chocolate until combined. Let sit for 15 more minutes at room temperature. Pour over cheesecake. Garnish with more chopped and toasted macadamia nuts, if desired.

Printed in the United States
By Bookmasters